MYTHS AND TALES FROM THE WHITE MOUNTAIN APACHE

BY PLINY EARLE GODDARD

ANTHROPOLOGICAL PAPERS OF THE AMERICAN MUSEUM OF
NATURAL HISTORY Vol. XXIV, Part II

With mixed Apache images

THE AMERICAN MUSEUM OF NATURAL HISTORY

SCIENCE EDUCATION

NEW YORK PUBLISHED BY ORDER OF THE TRUSTEES 1919

MYTHS AND TALES FROM THE WHITE MOUNTAIN APACHE.

By Pliny Earle Goddard.

Introduction.

These myths and tales are the free translations of texts recorded in the dialect of the White Mountain Apache. The texts themselves with word for word translations follow as Part IV of the volume. They were recorded, with one exception, during the winter of 1910 as a part of the studies made in the Southwest under the yearly grant of Mr. Archer M. Huntington. The creation myth, secured from Noze, differs in important incidents from the versions given above from the San Carlos as well as from versions secured from other White Mountain Apache. It should not be assumed that these differences are tribal, it is more probable that they are individual, since forms from the San Carlos and Navajo are closely similar to each other.

The greater number of the remaining narratives were secured from the father of Frank Crockett, the interpreter employed. Several of these are ceremonial and religious in their character and probably would not have been given except for the son's influence. Two of these were later secured from San Carlos informants in more extended form but highly corroborative in their general agreement.

The main purpose in recording these narratives was to secure sufficient and varied connected texts in the dialect of the White Mountain Apache. As a collection of mythology and folklore it is probably far from complete. It is assumed, however, to be fairly representative.

Pliny Earle Goddard.

January, 1919.

CONTENTS.

Alchise (aka Alchesay), 1853-1928, chief of the White Mountain Apache

Creation Myth.[1]

There were many houses there. A maiden went from the settlement to the top of a high mountain[2] and came where the rays of the rising Sun first strike. She raised her skirt and the "breath" of the Sun entered her. She went up the mountain four mornings, and four times the breath of the Sun penetrated her. This girl who had never been married became pregnant and the people were making remarks about it.

She went up the mountain on four successive days and four days after that, eight days altogether, she gave birth to a child. Four days later, the child stood on its feet. His fingers and toes were webbed and he had neither eyebrows nor eyelashes and the hairs on his head were scattered, one in a place. His ears were round with only the openings. Everyone said he did not look like a man. After four more days he walked well and played with the other children.

His mother went again to the east and lay down under a place where water was dripping. The water fell into her as it dripped from the hanging algæ. She did this four times and became pregnant. After four days they all saw that her abdomen was enlarged and when she had been in that condition four days, eight days in all, she gave birth to another child.[3] When it was four days old it stood up and was able to walk well. Its appearance was like that of the first child. It had webbed hands and feet and was without hair. It had round ears with holes only. The children walked about together, the head of one being higher than that of the other.

The people were asking, "Whose children are these going about?" They wanted to know who would make them like human beings. "Who are the kin of the woman whose children are going about among us?" The mother had a sister who wondered why the people were saying these things, for the boys had a father who lived a long way off.

The boys were eight days old and big enough to run about and were becoming intelligent. They asked their mother where their father was living. "Why do you ask?" she said. "You cannot go to him." "Why do you say that? Why do you hide our father from us?" the boys asked.

"Well, do you really want to go where your father lives?" she asked them. "Why do you suppose we are asking?" the boys replied. "We will go where our father lives." Their mother told them that they were talking foolishly, that the distance was great, and that they would not be able to go. The boys insisted but were again discouraged by their mother. They finally said that it must be they had no father if they could not go to him. The mother then consented and said they three would go to the top of a great mountain. She cut a supply of meat and after four days, when it was near dawn, they started. They came to the top of the mountain when it was day and stood there facing the Sun. The woman stood between the boys holding them by the hand. When the sun was rising she said: "Look, your father is rising. Observe well. His breath streams out from four sides. Go towards the streaming out of his breath. There are dangerous things living in the east. What have you to go with?" She had a brown fly and she gave it to the boys that it might sit by their ears. The fly was to show them the way and tell them where the dangerous ones lived.

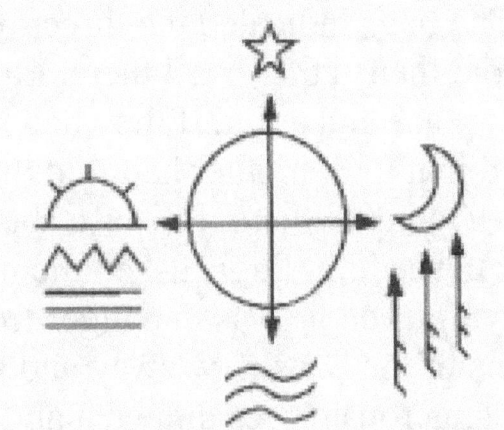

She told them they were to start at midday. They remained there until the sun reached the sky hole.[4] They then went four times around the trees on top of the mountain. The woman started home and the boys set out on their journey.

The boys went toward the east but the Sun was going in the opposite direction.[5] The boys sat down and cried. A Raven, spreading out his wings, alighted nearby and asked the boys why they were crying. The boys replied that their father lived over there and that they were going to visit him. The Raven asked if they were carrying anything in the way of food with them. They replied that they had some meat. The Raven said they might ride on his back if they would give him some of the meat. The fly told them it would be all right to ride on the Raven, that the Raven could see half the way and that there someone was living who knew the remainder of the way. They were told by the Raven to break up the meat and put the pieces in his mouth, that two of the parcels would sustain him until he finished the journey as far as he knew the way. They were directed to get on the Raven's back. The Raven began by flying near the ground, then went higher and higher, circling around. A hot rain fell but the Raven covered them with his wings. They kept putting the meat into the Raven's mouth. When they had fed the Raven two pieces of the meat they passed through a cloud where the large Eagle lived. The Raven told them that that one (the Eagle) would now take them, that he knew all the places because he saw everything upon the earth; that he himself would go back.

The Eagle asked them where they were going, saying that he lived in a dangerous place. The boys indicated the direction they were going, saying they had been told their father lived there. Eagle said it was true their father lived at that place and asked if they had heard about his house. The boys replied that their mother had told them that the Sun was their father and that he lived over there. Because she had told them this they were on their way to see him. Eagle asked them by what means they intended to go, saying even he was in danger from the Sun. The fly staying by the ear of one of the boys flew away and soon returned with the statement that the dangerous places did exist and that Eagle, with whom they were sitting, was the one who knew and was in control of these dangerous places. Before the house of the Sun was ice, interlocked like fallen timber. Eagle addressed the boys, asking if they had with them anything from the earth, meaning meat. They replied that they had and each of the boys took some from his pocket. Eagle asked for some of it, which when it was given him he ate.

Eagle then said they would set out, for he knew the trail. He requested them to put meat in his mouth as he flew with them, indicating the amount which would be sufficient, for the trail. When they were seated on the Eagle he started down with them, circling around as he flew. A storm of hail fell on them, the hailstones being large with thirty-two points.[6] The eagle protected the boys by covering them with his wings which were rolled back over them. When they had passed through the storm Eagle asked that meat be put in his mouth. When he had been fed he flew away with the boys and went through a hole which was there for him. When he came to the trail he alighted and pointing out the path told them that it led to the house of the Sun.[7] He said that he himself would now turn back home.

The boys went forward until they crossed a shallow valley beyond which was the house, which had projections running out in four directions. When they walked with their eyes closed the house went out of sight, but when they opened their eyes the house settled down again. It did this four times and then it stood firmly. The two boys walked on and coming to the house, stood in front of the entrance. An old woman who was the wife of the Sun sat there.

She advised them to go on wherever they were intending to go, since a person of mean disposition was soon to arrive. The woman who spoke to them was really handsome but she sat there in the form of an old woman. The boys replied that they had been told that their father lived there, and that they had started to come that morning. The woman replied that she did not know who their father was. The boys said that the Sun was their father and they had come to visit him. The woman then asked who had told them that the Sun was their father. They said their mother had told them so. The woman told them that their father would soon return and asked them to be seated on a chair she indicated. When they were seated, the chair kept whirling around with them. When the chair would lift up the woman would make it come down again. When the woman saw the chair come down again she announced herself as nearly convinced they had spoken the truth.

Saying that the Sun was now coming close, she took four silk blankets[8] of different colors which had been sewed together projecting in four directions and rolled the boys up in them. She put them into an inside room. They heard the Sun come back and heard him speak. "Old woman, where are the two men who came here?" he asked. The woman replied: "I have not seen anyone. No one has been here." "You say there is no one. They must have come, for here are their tracks," the Sun replied. "You must have been cohabiting with someone else. You say you travel over this broad earth and that you do not visit anyone. You must have been deceiving me about it for two men came in from that trail saying they are your children," his wife said. The Sun asked that they be brought in, and the woman opened the door, brought in the roll of blankets, and threw it down. The Sun shook the blankets and two men stood up. The Sun spoke: "Hesh, do you consider these to be my children? They do not look like me." He stood by them and repeated his question, calling attention to their webbed hands and feet and their round ears. "Are you really my children?" he asked them. "Who is called the Sun, I wonder?" the youngest of the boys said, and water fell from his eyes. "Well, maybe you are my children. Sit here and wait," the Sun said. Their fly looked around and reported that the man was their father. After examining the room everywhere, the inner corners, the windows, and door, the fly told them that ordeals were being prepared for them. He said that soon a blazing sky would be arranged, into which they would be thrown. The fly looked around for downy feathers which he gave the boys.

When the Sun had finished eating he asked that those who said they were the Sun's children should be brought in. He threw them into the place of danger. He pushed them in with lightning which had sharp spines. They turned into downy feathers and stood in front of him again. "It is true," the Sun said. He threw them in four times, pushing them down. Each time they turned into feathers and came back in front of the Sun as before. The Sun then said he was convinced that they were his children. His wife said: "They told you they were your children, but you have treated them badly." The Sun replied: "They certainly are my children but I did not believe it before." The Sun asked his wife to prepare a sweatlodge as soon as they had eaten.

She made a sweatlodge covered with a blue blanket on one side, a black one on another side, a white one on another side, and a yellow one on another side. His wife had the stones heated red hot, like red hot iron. They three went right in, but the Sun only came out again. When the bath had been heated the fourth time the boys were as if they had been boiled. He pushed back the skin which was between their fingers and toes. He fixed for them their lower leg muscles, their knees, their thighs, their biceps, their elbows, and their lower arms. He made the hair of their heads come to their hips, twisting it off at that length. He made their ears, their eyelashes, and their eyebrows, their noses, their mouths, and their faces. He fixed every part of their bodies as it should be. The Sun went out of the bath with the boys and sat with them on the seat where his wife usually sat. They were just like men.[9] When the wife of the Sun came and stood in front of them she looked at them closely, but could not distinguish one from the other. "Move, husband," she said. The one sitting in the middle moved himself. "You told me you had not been with any woman but you fooled me. These are your children. You must have a wife. Go home with them," the woman said.

The Sun spoke to his wife, saying that these were his children but that if he went away with them to the earth she would be lonesome. Only today there was a good sunset. "Just now when you said 'no' your eye winked," he said to her. "I am jealous of what is far away," she said. The Sun said he would not go, but would talk to his children.

"My boys, shall I give you names?" "Yes, it is not well to be without names," they replied. Then the Sun said he would name them. He told the older his name would be Naiyenezgani and that he must behave well.[10] He told the other one that he would be named Tobatc'istcini. "When you are upon the earth you will be called so and you will tell them that your father named you that. You shall say, 'He made my name Naiyenezgani.' But you, 'Tobatc'istcini he made my name,' you must tell them."

The Sun then asked them for what they had come. They told him they had come for his horse, his saddle, his bridle, his halter, his rope, and his saddle blanket. The Sun asked who had told them he had such property. The older one replied that their mother had told them what property he had and had told them that she would be happy if they brought it back to the earth. She said that he (the Sun) would also be happy. The Sun replied that he had no property, no horse, saddle, bridle, halter, rope, or saddle blanket. The fly had told them that the Sun had these, but he looked around again and reported that the Sun had them close by.

"Let us go over there," one of them proposed. They went to a fenced enclosure and entered through a gate. The yard was so full of black bears that the mass of their moving backs occupied the entire space. "Which of those are my horses?" the Sun asked. "They are fearful animals," the boys replied. "These are my horses," the Sun insisted and mounted one of them and rode around on it. The fly informed the boys that they were being deceived. The Sun proposed that they should go in another direction to another enclosure. Inside this yard were white-tail deer, mule deer, elk, and mountain-sheep. The Sun announced that these were his horses and told the boys to choose any one they liked and catch it. "Which is the largest?" he asked them. "These are not horses," the boys replied, "they are named deer. We asked you for horses." The Sun insisted they were his horses and that he rode them great distances. "Well, you have outwitted me. I thought I would succeed in outwitting you, but you have won." The younger brother asked the Sun what he was concealing from them, saying he could find them. The Sun asked them not to say that and proposed that they look in another place where he had a few horses confined. They went to the place indicated and found the place filled with antelope, sheep, goats, and pigs. "Catch any one of these you want," the Sun said. "You tend to them here alone," the boys replied and walked out leaving the Sun who followed behind.

They went to the house and ate a meal. Their fly told them that the Sun's horses were in the enclosure that had four doors. When they had finished eating they went to this enclosure which was a house with a roof having holes in it. It had spikes like irons, sticking up from it. It was closed and completely dark. "There are horses in there," the fly told them. The Sun said, "I told you it was useless." One of the boys asked that they might look in. There was a door there which he opened. A little beyond it was another door, a little beyond another, and a little beyond that another, and still beyond that another. They now came to horses in the enclosure but could not enter. By standing on something they could see through a hole in the roof. They could not get in between the horses until they were caused to separate and to open up a passage. The Sun then told them to catch the horse that they thought was his. The fly sitting by one of their ears told them they were to catch the horse with a rope which they should induce the Sun to give them. When the Sun again urged them to catch the horse without delay, they asked whether they should lead the horse by the mane or carry him out in their hands. The Sun, with spotted ropes in his hand, went right through the door which he opened. He gave one of the ropes to each of the boys, telling them to catch the horses which were his. The animals were milling around in the enclosure. In the center was one which was not moving, a sorrel with a small white spot on its forehead. Its mane reached the ground. When it raised its head one of the boys started toward it, the horses separating. He threw the rope and caught the horse which he led back. The Sun then told the other boy to catch a horse, wanting to know who had told him which horse to catch. There was a stallion running around the outside of the herd. Its mane reached the ground; he was acting wild but the fly told them that although he acted as if he were mean he was really gentle. He directed them to take both these horses from the Sun. When the other boy started with his rope toward the stallion he was running around the outside of the herd and coming toward the boy. When he came close and saw the boy he stopped and then wheeled back. The boy lassoed it and immediately the horse trotted up to him, nosing his arm. He led the stallion up beside the sorrel horse which was a mare. The Sun said: "There they are, ride them, take them with you to the earth."

The boys then asked for the horse trappings for which they had also come. The Sun said he did not know what they meant by horse trappings. The younger boy said, "Well, if you do not know what horse trappings are, do not again put them on these horses in the corral." The Sun asked who it was who had made them as smart as he was himself. They replied that he, the Sun, had made them smart and had made them speak wisely. They then asked by name for bridle, halter, saddle blanket, and saddle.[11] Turning his back to the boys he walked away and opened a door, bidding the boys enter. They went in and saw saddles lying there with bridles hanging on the saddle horns. The blankets were lying beneath. Before they went in the fly flew in and selected two out of all the saddles. One was lying at the east and the other at the west. The first was blue and the other yellow. The fly had returned to one of their ears by the time the Sun said: "There are those saddles, take the ones you want." The fly told the boys that the saddles which looked good really were not, but that they should choose the blue and yellow ones, indicating them, and the blankets, halters, bridles, and ropes of similar colors lying by them. These were the Sun's own particular set of trappings. When the Sun urged them to hurry up each boy stepped toward the saddle he had chosen. When they did so the saddles moved of themselves with the blankets and bridles. There was a sound "gij" of the moving leather and "tsil" as they came to rest.

Apache girl with basket

The Sun turned his face away and took a black silk handkerchief which had two white stripes around the border from his pocket. With this he wiped his eyes. "I raised you for just this purpose," he said. The

Sun started to walk toward the horses. Their fly had told them not to touch the saddles, that the Sun himself would fix them. "They belong to you," the fly said. "Everything is alive; the rope on the horse moves about of itself. The saddle will jump on of itself."[12] The fly told them this. The halter was gone, the bridle and saddle blanket which had been lying on the saddle were gone. The halter, bridle, and saddle blanket that had been with the blue saddle were also gone. The Sun called them to come where he was standing. They both went out again and the doors of the saddle room and of the stable were shut.

They went to the Sun, who was standing between the two horses so that their heads projected as he held the bridles. They started away, the boys walking in front of the Sun as he directed them to do. They passed through the four doors to a post standing in front of the Sun's house. He led the horses to the post where they stood without being tied.[13] There were four chairs standing inside the Sun's house; and one by itself for the woman.[14] His children sat on the chairs and his wife sat on the one which was hers. The Sun addressed them as follows:—

"My boys, I will instruct you about the dangerous places you will come to. The horses know the dangerous places on the way back. My wife is pleased with you and treats you well. That is why you are to have these horses, one of which is hers. The other is mine and so is the saddle, bridle, halter, and saddle blanket. They are all mine. You will go back to your kindred. When you are near, hurry. I will give you something."

The Sun got up and reached inside to a shelf from which he took up an iron knife like a sword. Turning around he took up a bow and arrows having iron heads. There were two of the arrows. "I give these to you," he said. "You are giving us these! Our mother did not know about them. Why does she not give us something?" the boys said. The Sun's wife said she would speak a few words to them. "You shall be my nephews. Your mother shall be my sister. She shall be like me. Because of this I have treated you well. She shall be the same as I. I become an old woman and at other times I am as if I were two years old. She shall be the same way.[15] You shall tell her this before the Sun travels far. I am the one telling you; he did not tell you. I will name my sister. Your father will give you names." The Sun picked something up and was still holding it. "Wait, I will tell you something and after that he will give you a name. I name her Nigostsanbikayo.[16] Everyone will call her that. She will come to me. You, too, will come to me. I give a name to your mother. She will be called Ests'unnadlehi and she will help you. I make a name for her, Ests'unnadlehi, and with that she will help you. When she has children again they will be two girls. These girls will belong to the people for there will be people.[17] She will help them. I, too, will help them when they come to me. He, too, will help his children. That is why I am telling you and you must remember it well. I have finished. Your father will tell you about the objects he is about to give you."

The Sun gave the elder boy a weapon saying, "This will be called a 'blue sword.' You will use it against the monsters on the earth. Because of that I gave you the name, Naiyenezgani." He gave the weapon to him saying, "That is all for you." Addressing the younger, he said, "Now I give this to you, Tobatc'istcini. You will use this which I give you against those who prey upon people. You are to help each other. I shall be near you watching you. Whatever you do will be known to me. It will be well if you kill these evil ones. The people will live everywhere." He gave him the bow with the injunction that he should draw the bow three times without releasing the arrow and then he should shoot the dangerous beings and they would fly apart. Having said this, he proposed they should eat something. The Sun's wife was still sitting in her accustomed seat. The men went to the table, well loaded with food prepared by some unknown agency, and began to eat. The Sun's wife gave the elder one a spotted belt with a yellow fringe hanging from its border.

When they had finished the meal, the Sun said he did not know how the visitors were to return. They went where the horses stood and the Sun said, "Children, this stallion will go well in the lead. Now mount the horses." He held the stirrup and saddle horn and told the boys to get on. They did so and rode away from the Sun's house where towards the east a post stands up with white hair[18] which reaches to the ground and turns up again. The rain falls on it. They rode their horses around this post four times and came back where they were standing before, as the Sun directed them to do.

When they had finished, the Sun's wife came up to them and told her husband to count for his sons the two saddle blankets, two halters, two bridles, two ropes, and two saddles. The Sun told them to start home; that he was well acquainted with them. He charged them to take good care of the saddle blankets and directed that the gray horse should go in the lead because he knew the trail to the place midway between the earth and the sky. From that point the sorrel horse was to lead because that one knew the way from there on. When they returned where their mother lived he told them to stake the horses out for four nights. The sorrel was to be staked toward the east and the gray to the west. Having ridden the horses among the people they were to unsaddle them in some good place. A white saddle blanket was to be placed toward the east, a black one to the south, a yellow one to the west, and a blue one to the north.[19] The bridles, halters, ropes, and saddles were to be brought to the camp. He charged them to keep in mind what he was telling, for he was telling them this that they might be good men. He divided his property between his boys. He told them after the horses had been running loose four days to go to them early in the morning. This might be in any good place where canyons meet, making a flat. When they came to them they were to hold out their hands, palms upward, towards the horses. They were to catch the horses while they were licking their hands. They were to consider what he told them and when they should go for the horses after four days, the four canyons coming together would be full of horses. When their horses had been caught by holding out their hands, the saddle blankets, one on the other, were to be put on them and the horses were to be saddled. They were to ride the horses all day until sunset when they were to be turned out again. Having turned them out, they were told they might go the next day to see what was happening. Having finished his speech he dismissed the boys.

They went with the Sun until they came to the top of the ridge, where they stopped. The Sun felt the horses all over. He felt of their legs, their feet, their faces, their ears, their manes, their backs, petting them. "Goodbye, my horses," he said, "travel well for my boys down to the earth. There is food for you on the earth the same as here." He addressed the gray horse, telling him to be the leader on the way toward the earth since he knew the way. He told the boys not to look at the horses' feet nor to look behind them, but to keep their eyes fixed on the tips of their ears.

Apache women 1898

They started; before they knew it the horses had changed places, and the sorrel was leading. They thought the earth was far off but they soon found the horses were trotting along on the earth. Now the horses were running with them toward their camp. They rode up slowly where the people were walking about. They rode to the camp side by side, and the people all ran out to look at them. Their mother was standing outside watching them and they rode up one on each side of her. "Mother, Ests'unnadlehi, unsaddle our horses," they said to her.

The people all came up to them. The woman, laughing, ran her hand over the horses saying, "Your father gave you large horses." When the people had all come there, the boys told them to call their mother Ests'unnadlehi. They all called her by that name. The older boy said they were to call him Naiyenezgani. The younger one said they were to call him Tobatc'istcini.[20] They addressed them saying, "When we were here before you used to laugh at us because we were poor. We used to walk because we were poor. We have visited our father where he lives. The Sun's wife named our mother. Call me Naiyenezgani. That one was given the name, Tobatc'istcini. These will be our names and be careful to call them correctly. Do not come near these horses. We will stake one out here and the other one there. They will remain tied out four days. You may go."

Before sundown on the fourth day the horses whinnied. They went to their horses and saddled them. They rode around among the camps until sundown and then rode them to a flat where four canyons came together. They hung a white saddle blanket toward the east, a black one to the south, a yellow one to the west, and a blue one to the north. Their fly told them to hang the blankets in four places, making an enclosure of them. After four days they were to come and would find conditions different. He charged the boys not to miss doing just as their father had told them. They went back to the camp carrying the saddles, bridles, halters, and ropes. After two days had passed their fly flew away. He returned, reporting that there were many horses filling the place where the four canyons came together. The next day he reported that the horses were so thick one could walk on their backs. The next day (the fourth), about sunrise, the two boys went there with their ropes in their hands. When they came to the eastern canyon it was full of white horses, the southern one was full of black horses, the western was full of yellow horses, and the northern canyon with blue (gray) horses.

They took down all the saddle blankets and piled them together. With valleys in four directions full of horses they did not know their former horses from the others. They considered how they might distinguish them. The horses were milling around near where a blanket hung. They were all mingled together with the colors mixed. The men approached the horses but they stopped before they got to them. They extended their hands with pollen on the palms and the horses whinneyed. Then two horses trotted up to them and licked the pollen from the hands of their owners who caught them while they did it.[21] They led these horses back to the camp where the saddles, etc., were lying.

When they led these two horses all the others followed. Their fly told them all about the two horses, what they had done, and that they had made many horses for them. Four days from now it would come about that the broad earth would be covered with horses. Their fly flew to the Sun's camp and the Sun instructed him. "Drive the horses over this way and put a halter on top of that mountain; put a rope on the top of this mountain to the south; put a halter on the top of the mountain to the west; and put a rope on the mountain to the north. Your father says this," the fly told them.

The older of the brothers told the people that they should ride the horses and not think they were wild. "Catch any of them and saddle them. When you have ridden your horses, then do not go near them for four days. Keep away from the horses which are inside where the halters and ropes are lying. Turn the horses loose in the space enclosed by the ropes and the halter. If they see you they may stampede. These horses will be of great value to you."

The brothers rode the two horses and the others all followed. When the two horses whinneyed, the others all answered. They took off the ropes and went back to camp. They asked their mother to put up two posts and to put a smooth pole across their tops. She was asked to put the saddles on this pole with their horns toward the east.[22] The bridles were to be hung on the saddle horns and the saddle blankets spread over the saddles. They asked her to think about the saddles where they were lying during the night.

She kept her mind on the saddles during the night and in the early morning she went out to them. There were four saddles on the pole where there had been only two. She still kept her mind on the saddles and the next morning there were six lying there. "My child," she said, "you spoke the truth. I kept my mind on the saddles and six are now lying there." Tobatc'istcini said, "Very well, keep thinking about them all night and go to them early in the morning." When she went out, there were eight saddles on the pole.

Naiyenezgani said he was going yonder and would be back by sunset. He went to the mountain top where the halter lay. The Sun was standing there. "It must be my father," he said. "I did not know you. I am glad you came down to me." "Well, my son," the Sun replied, "let us go around the horses." "What time will it be when we get around them?" the son asked. Leaving the place where the halters were lying they went where the ropes were. The space was level full of horses. "Fine, my son," the Sun said to Naiyenezgani, "with ropes and halters you made a fence so the horses cannot get out. You have this broad world for a corral."

They went on and came where the halters were piled up. "These halters will round up the wild horses for you and you will put them on their heads." They went on and came where the rope hung. "These ropes will drive the horses together for you. They will drive the wild horses close to camp for you." They started back and came where Naiyenezgani had met the Sun. "I have done everything for you," the Sun said. "Now I am going back and leave you. You too will go home. Tomorrow it will be finished. You will give your people two horses apiece. Give each of them one stallion and one mare. Distribute them from noon until sunset. These horses are mares and stallions in equal numbers. Tonight two saddles are to be placed on the pole you put up. You shall keep three saddles and give away seven. When you give away the horses give away seven saddles. Now my son, we separate. Shake hands. Others will do as we do." They said *njo* to each other and separated. It was not long before he was back and stood there as the sun set. He was happy and laughing. "Where have you been, my son?" his mother asked. "You must have been in a good place or you would not be laughing." "What did you say, mother?" he replied. "I am happy; when I came over there where the halter lay I met my father. I walked with him all day. As we walked around the horses he told me about everything. I am happy."

He said that none of them should go out tomorrow, but that he himself would go out early. When he went out there in front of the yellow saddle lay a white saddle. Behind that was a blue one. Between them was a yellow saddle. The pole was full. There were ten saddles in a row. "I told you to put up a long pole, and you put up a short one," he said to his mother. "You said dig one hole here and another there, my son," she replied. "Just these may well be our saddles," he said. He called Tobatc'istcini, saying they would go to catch the horses. "You go to the rope over there. I, too, will go to the other rope. Hurry, we will catch the horses," he said to him. He ran where one rope was, and the other one went where the other rope was. When they came to the two ropes, they circled around, driving the horses all towards each other. They could not find their own horses, the Sun's horses. They went into the enclosure and walked around. Even when they went around that way they could not find the horses. They looked for them again, going around among the other horses, but they could not find them. The horses touched each other, they were so thick.

Then Tobatc'istcini said, "Naiyenezgani, why do you act so? Is your mind gone? You say you met your father yesterday and that you spent the day going around the horses. He took them out of the herd, and away from you."

Geronimo

Naiyenezgani caught a black stallion and the other brother a sorrel gelding. When they led them to the camp their mother asked Tobatc'istcini why he had caught a sorrel and told him to turn him loose and catch a white gelding. She said the gray and sorrel horses were made for them and that they were well trained the day before. She told them to hurry and drive the horses in. Tobatc'istcini rode the sorrel horse back and unsaddled it. He then caught a white horse and drove the gray horses back to the camp.[23]

"Let us go," he said to his brother. They mounted the horses and rode along. Their mother spoke to them, "My boys, take off that yellow saddle and put on a white one." When they came riding back where their mother was, a horse whinneyed. It sounded like the voice of the gray stallion that used to be his horse. Another horse whinneyed in this direction and the voice was like that of the sorrel mare. They knew their horses when they whinneyed and one said to the other, "Brother, those are our horses whinneying but we cannot do anything about it."[24] "Let us hurry," the other said. They rode toward the herd of horses but the horses started to run and the herd broke up. While they were looking they ran where their horses whinneyed. Their fly told them that the horses had already run into the enclosure and that the four doors were shut. They heard them whinneying far away. Their fly said the horses were already in their stable, but they still whinneyed. They drove the other horses near the camp. The older brother told the people to form in a line around the horses. He said they were going to stake out horses for them. The people replied that they had no ropes, that only the two brothers had them. They asked the brothers to make ropes for them. They were told to wait while they returned where the horses used to be. They told them that they would have ropes the next day. The brothers went in different directions, calling to each other. They met and sent their fly to the Sun because the people were without ropes. He told his brother to go back where he had been staying. He directed him also to take the bridle off and to leave the rope as it was, tied to the saddle. "When the Sun is in the middle of the sky we will drive the horses back. Although it is late the Sun will be in the same place.[25] He (the Sun) may give us something," he said.

The fly returned and reported: "Your horse was standing behind him. He sat watching where the stallions were fighting each other. He kept looking at them and then he went a little way."

The Sun's disk was yellow as at sunset. He looked down four times. The yellow beams struck under his raised knees. From the other side they also streamed toward him. Nothing happened, and he got up and went to his horse. When he put his foot in the stirrup and mounted, ropes were tied in four places to the saddle strings where there had been no ropes before. Both saddles were that way. They both mounted together and their horses pawed the ground and snorted. He rode back to the camp, loping, and the other horses strung out behind him. The other brother was running his horse on the other side. They stopped near the camp. The horses were all lined up facing him. He called to the one on horseback, "Come here." He rode up to him and he asked how many ropes there were. The other replied he did not know for he had not counted them, and inquired of the other how many ropes he had. The first speaker replied that he did not know. Then the younger brother said the other should catch the horses for them and lead them out while he remained on his horse where he was. The other brother then rode among the horses and caught a mare. He led the horse out and gave the rope to one of the men. He rode back among the horses and caught a stallion. When he had caught six horses, the ropes were all gone. He beckoned with his hand and his brother rode up to him. "Had you only six ropes?" he asked. "Yes, I only had six and I have caught six horses. Now, take your turn and I will remain here on horseback." The second brother caught the horses and reported that he had chosen the better horses. The horses were all good but some of them looked to be small.

They told the people there were only seven saddles and that so many of the men might have saddles, but that the others must ride around bareback for the present. He told them that sometime they might have saddles because the Sun knew of their need and he himself knew it. He instructed them to tie out their horses close by. He said if they heard the horses nickering they would know that the stallions were covering the mares. They would also know the colts when they were foaled. If they turned their horses loose they might not know them. The ropes he said would guard their horses for them. They would now drive back the other horses while those who had received horses staked theirs out.

He drove the horses away and hung his bridle up. The other one he laid in another direction. He took the saddle and everything else back to the camp. They came back to the camp in the middle of the night but they did not know it was night because the Sun had not moved.

When two days had passed two men came. There were many horses where they had passed. They reported that something was running around the other side of this large mountain. They did not know what it was, nor to whom it belonged. They wondered what was meant and sent their fly to find out. He flew away and came back almost immediately. He said it was true. On the ridge beyond the mountain he saw horse tracks and a trail with dust as fine as flour.

Jicarilla Apache

One of the brothers asked his mother to cook for the men quickly. It was while they were eating that the fly reported. "Fly back there," he directed him. He told the visitors to remain, for they were no doubt tired. They went back where the bridle was lying. They took off the rope and hung it toward the east. They spoke to the bridle asking that the horses, wherever they went, should come back together during the night.

The visitors were as the two brothers had been. They had no eyelashes or eyebrows. Their ears were round and their heads were smooth. There were webs between their fingers and toes. When they were asked whence they came they replied that they had assumed there were people living somewhere. Their own people had been killed off by something until only the two were left. They saved themselves at night by digging a trench and covering it with a large rock. When they started away, one of the brothers asked where they were going. They replied that they did not know where they were going but preferred not to stay where they were. They said they did not like to be with many peoples. They preferred staying there with their present hosts. Naiyenezgani asked them to tell their story during the night.

When night came, he called four men to come and listen to what the visitors were about to tell. He asked each of the four men to question the guests. "What is the country called where you live and what kind of thing is killing your people?" he asked. "Tell us about it."

"The place where we live is called *danagogai*, plain. Something has been killing our kinsfolk. It has been killing people everywhere on the earth. We do not know what to do," one of them replied. Naiyenezgani told another of the men to question them. He asked if it were really true that they had been living in that place, saying he did not believe what the other had said. One of the guests replied that it was true. He said they did not know how to tell untruths and that it was not right to do so. "While we are here in camp it will kill someone." He added, "I have finished." The second questioner said, "Why did you tell us this? We are uneasy about it." They replied that they were afraid of it and therefore came there where they intended to live with them.

Naiyenezgani called upon a third man to question them. "Why did you leave a trail for them?" he inquired. "When your kinsfolk were all killed, why did you come to us leaving a trail?" The same man spoke again. He directed that the next day a sweatbath should be prepared that they should take a bath with the two visitors.

"You said the horses had gone far away. I presume they have already come together again," he said. "These some-kind-of-things you said were going away we call horses. That is all I have to say." "These two will speak to you," one of the company said.

"I cannot promise that I will kill that thing which has been killing your people. Hurry to build the sweatlodge he mentioned," Tobatc'istcini said. "Make the sweatbath: we are going for the horses," he added.

During the night the horses had come together. One bridle was lying at the east and the other at the west. They told the horses they must all stay there together. When the brothers returned the sweatlodge was built and the stones were on the fire. Tobatc'istcini directed that the men should stand in line while four of them should go into the bath four times. He said that when they had come out the fourth time the visitors would be like themselves. "You built this sweatbath, but it belongs to the Sun," he told them. When he (Naiyenezgani) went in with them the fourth time he asked them where the thing was living which was killing them. The visitors replied that he lived down this way, pointing toward the west. "The one that has killed all of our people has something long for a weapon," he added. Naiyenezgani said, "Well, he has been killing you." When they came out the fourth time they all looked alike. They ate and after the meal the brothers told them all to remain there while they went to yonder white mountain ridge to look beyond. He looked at the Sun.

They landed far away on the mountain ridge.[26] Beyond that mountain they went to another. There was a plain on which a mountain was standing. They landed next on that mountain. Tobatc'istcini said, "Brother, is the dangerous thing feared by you? If you are afraid, I am afraid. If you are not afraid neither am I afraid. You are the elder, I am the younger."

A man was walking in a valley without brush. He was the one who kills people. They sent their fly to look over the body of their enemy, to examine his ears, his eyes, and his mouth. The fly flew to the man and alighted on his ear. When he alighted on his nose the man said, "It is not just you. You smell like a man."

The fly reported that they could not come up to the man, for while he walked in one direction he could see behind because he had eyes in the back of his head. He had no eyes in front. "He has something long in his hand with which he kills people. When I sat on his nose he told me I smelled like people," the fly reported. "He is the same sort of a person that you are." The fly told them to go around to a certain gap in the ridge, where the monster was accustomed to pass, and stand side by side. He promised to let them know when the enemy approached. When the monster walked along, the fly came back where the brothers were standing side by side and said, "He is coming up here very close. If he stops here you must cut his head off. Now, you shoot him," he said. "If he sees anyone he makes a sweep with his long weapon and kills the person even a long way off."

The man came close to them and stopped. One of them shot him and the other cut his head off. He stood just as he was before. They shot again and cut his head off again. The head fell but came back on again. One of them shot at him the third time and the other cut his neck off again. Then one of them ran around in front of him and shot him in the heart. This time his flesh flew apart and was scattered over considerable space. The flesh was quivering. That which they killed was called Naiye'. "That is why he named you Naiyenezgani,"[27] their fly said. "Because you and Tobatc'istcini both will kill dangerous beings your father named you that." "You did this in his presence. He was looking at you and prevented the monster's making any move against you. He gave you the weapons with which you killed him. He did it for the good of mankind. Turn the head over and look at its face," their fly told them. They turned him over and looked at his face. His face was like anyone's but he also had eyes in the back of his head.[28] No one could attack him from in front, and he had eyes to see behind himself also. His knife was sharp and the handle was good. "Let us take the knife to convince the people. If we do not have the knife, they will not believe us if we claim we have killed the Naiye' which used to kill people," one of them said.

On their return they landed on the white mountain ridge and returned to the camp. When they had returned, Naiyenezgani directed that all the people, including the children, should come together. He asked his mother, because the people were assembling, to spread down a buckskin and to place on it the arrows, his own weapon, and that of the slain Naiye'. He asked the people to gather around it. He called the two visitors, asking them to come to a designated spot. He told his brother to stand in a certain position and said that he himself would stand in another place. He said that he would address the people and told his brother to do the same. "I am telling you this because you are seeing what you have not seen before. You see today what our father gave us. Now you speak to them," he said to his brother.

Tobatc'istcini spoke as follows, "My name is Tobatc'istcini. Our father gave us these things lying here. A being called Naiye' was using that weapon over there to kill people. He had killed all the people except the two who are sitting over there. We killed him." "You, Naiyenezgani, speak to them again," he said to his brother.

Cochise

"We started from here and we went up to the top of yonder mountain. We went on to the top of a mountain standing beyond that. A small mountain[29] stands beyond that and we went up to its top. There we saw a man walking in a valley. He[30] went to him for us and returned. 'When he walks he is blind, but he has eyes in the back of his head,' he reported to us. 'He kills the people who are slipping up behind him.' Now he will not kill anyone. We shall live safely." He took up what used to be his knife and carried it around for the people to see. The man's blood was on it, and it was fearful to look at. "There is no place to take hold of it. I will take hold of it here," he said. "Do not look at this which used to belong to Naiye'. It is dangerous. Have a meal and then go home. Look after our horses well."

Their mother asked why the two who had come to them should not accompany them where the horses were. They went with them where the horses were. "Catch the sorrel gelding when you want to. You can tell it by the white spot on its shoulder," he told one of them. To the other he said, "You may catch this black one with a white spot on its forehead. If we are away anywhere saddle them and ride them around among the horses and through the camp. The horses look as if they were mean, as if they had never had a rope on them, but they will not misbehave, they are not mean and will not shy." They started back and when they came to the camp again they ate.

Two days after they had killed the Naiye' they said they were going in a certain direction and that it might be late when they returned. They went up to the top of a small sharp-topped mountain. They looked at the Sun and, when it came up, yellow beams streamed out from the Sun's disk. His breath took the shape of a rainbow. The sunbeams fell to the ground over them. "It must be there," he said. They started and landed on a mountain top. From there they went to another and from that one to a projecting ridge. Beyond that was a plain on which stood a blue mountain. They landed on that. It seems that those who were killing the people lived at a distance from each other and the people were living in the center of the world. The killers of the people were working towards each other.

The two brothers stood on the mountain side by side. They were made like their father. You could hardly see their bodies. They were killing out the Naiye'. "Fly over the country and hunt him up. He is living somewhere," one of them said to the fly. It flew off and went around them in a circle. The next time it went around in a smaller circle. He (the monster) was coming behind them. He had eyes looking both ways, four eyes. He held something crooked. He stopped and looked carefully behind himself. He did not look in front. He could look straight up and could see people down below. The fly looked him all over, at his eyes, his ears, his nose, and his face. "You are a burr," he said to the fly. The fly thought he said he was going to catch him. He flew between the man's legs and returned where the brothers were sitting. "Did you say Naiye'? You have come to a dangerous place," the fly said to them. "As he walks along he looks carefully behind himself. When he stops he looks up and he can see the people who are below.[31] He carries a long, crooked object with which he makes a sweep at people he sees in the distance and catches them with his hook."

The fly was sent again to find out from which point the monster could be attacked with the best chances for success. They saw him walking in the distance and then they saw him standing where he was accustomed to come up the ridge. The fly reported that was a good place for the attack. The brothers addressed each other. "What is the matter with you, Tobatc'istcini?" Naiyenezgani asked. "You are the leader and should speak first," Tobatc'istcini replied. "Very well, you did not answer me. We will attack him. I will cause large hail with thirty-two points to fall on him. What are you going to do?" Naiyenezgani asked. "I will cause hot rain to fall on him," was the reply.

They went to him where he was walking. The sky made a noise and it began to rain. The two brothers came toward him behind this rain. He put his hand to the top of his head. It was hot rain which was falling. They could see him, but he could not see them. "Let him walk between you," the fly directed. He was already exhausted with the hot rain and the hail. Naiyenezgani stood here and Tobatc'istcini there. The monster walked here saying, "It is a bad time. I, too, where I am, it is a bad place." As he walked one of the brothers raised his bow and brought it down again, shooting. His companion cut off the monster's head. It came back immediately as it was before. They shot and cut his head off again. He fell three ways. They did the same thing to him the fourth time and he spread out like water. "There shall not be those who kill," Naiyenezgani said. "This is the way I do to Naiye'. Just let him float here in his blood. The people will live happily on the earth. I have done well by them. Get ready, brother, we will go back. We will take the weapon with which he has been killing people." He rolled this weapon up into a coil and put it in his blanket. "Come, we will go back," he said.

They came back in the manner they went, landing on the successive mountains until they reached the camp. They danced a war dance near the camp. They danced, holding up the weapon they had taken. "Mother, we are hungry, hurry and cook for us," they said to her. When they had eaten they asked their mother to assemble the people and to ask the visitors also to come. She told the people to assemble, saying that her sons must have seen something during the day they had been away which they would tell them about. When the people had come together the weapon they had brought back was lying there, not as yet untangled.

"We killed one like the other one. We both did it, but I could have done it by myself, if I had been alone. If he had been alone he too could have done it by himself," Naiyenezgani said. "We both attacked him because we could do it quickly. We killed him quickly because our father helped us. If it had been one of you, you could have done nothing with this one that we call Naiye'. He would have killed you right away and eaten you up. He had killed all the people who lived with these two men, and just now he was coming for you. Before we had known it, he would have killed us all. There are no people living on the edges of the earth. We are all that are left. He killed people this way. Suppose that person should come on you, he would kill you this way." He threw the weapon to a distant bush. It went around the tree and it was as if it had been cut off. "He was killing people thus. Now we will live well and no one will bother us. A man is going around the earth in one day and he will tell us about it."[32] Tobatc'istcini started away and his mother spoke to him. "My son, put on this belt," she said, offering him the one the Sun's wife had given her. "I am going around from here but today it is late, I will go tomorrow," he said. They went to bed. "Take good care of things and do not be afraid of anything," Tobatc'istcini said.

When it was daylight their mother prepared a meal for them and they ate. "Come back safely, my son, as the people said to you," the mother said. "I am going, but I do not know when I shall come back," Tobatc'istcini replied. He started, telling them to watch for him on a certain mountain point. "I will be back about noon."

He started away, traveling with a blue flute which had wings.[33] He went with this from place to place and was back home before long. He went entirely around the border of the world on which people were living. The belt was a blue flute. He thought with it four ways and looked into it four ways. Before noon a light rain fell on the projecting mountain. That cleared off and then he came laughing. "It was not far, only so large," he said, joining the tips of his forefinger and his thumb. "Have you your property ready?" he asked. "Have you collected everything that is ours? Tomorrow we will give out the horses, one apiece to each of you. We shall not give out horses again. Bring the horses near to the camp."

They brought the saddles, the bridles, the halters, the ropes, and the blankets. They two went where the horses were. They caught some of the horses and saddled them, and drove the other horses near the camp where they herded them. They called the people to assemble and when they came caught horses for them. He gave away ten horses in all. "I will give you no more horses," he said. "Tomorrow we will go different ways."[34] He drove the horses back where they stayed. "Stake out our horses nearby and leave the saddles on them all night," he said. "This is all. You may go in any direction you like." "This way," pointing to the east; "this way," south; "this way," west; or "this way," north. "We are going over here where the end of the world is," some of them said. Others said they were going to the end of the world in this direction. In this manner, each party chose a location.

Apache Woman

When they had finished, they asked the brothers which way they were going. They replied that they were going to drive their horses to the top of yonder mountain (*bitsanldai*). "Take good care of your horses. Look after them for twelve days and then they will be accustomed to you. Now you may go. We are going also." He drove his horses away saying, "None of you are going with us. I thought some of you would go with us. You are only giving us back our mother. Go on, mother, let your horse lead."

His mother inquired which way she should lead them. "Go on, go on, I tell you," he replied. She rode towards the east. Soon a little light was to be seen under the horse. They went higher and higher until they came to the mountain he spoke of. They rode their horses beside hers. "Wait, mother," he said and rode back. "Keep on down this mountain. It is good country in this basin. We will live here," he said. They talked together. "You unsaddle over there, you over there, and you over there. We will watch the horses."

"You may have my yucca fruit which lies on the face of Turnbull Mountain."[35]

1. Told by a White Mountain Apache called Noze, at Rice, Arizona, in January. 1910. Noze was a native of Cedar Creek and came to the San Carlos Reservation when it was organized. He was for a long time the chief of a considerable band which in 1910 had greatly dwindled. He died sometime between 1910 and the next visit in 1914.

2. This mountain was said to be called *tsidalanasi* and to stand by the ocean at the south. This is a remarkable statement as east would have been expected and as is so stated in fact in a following paragraph.

3. This makes the boys brothers in our use of the word. They are always so called in the Navajo account according to which their mothers were sisters. Matthews, 105.

4. At the center of the sky.

5. And therefore the boys were not seen by the Sun.

6. The sacred numbers are 4, 12, and 32.

7. This method of making the journey has not been encountered before in this connection, but is an incident in a European story secured from the San Carlos, p. 82, above. The usual account includes a series of obstacles some of which resemble the incidents of a European story. See p. 116 below.

8. Clouds according to the Navajo account, Matthews, 111; and below, p. 117.

9. Thus far the myth seems chiefly to deal with the adolescence ceremony of the boys. The San Carlos account brings in the Sun's father and brothers of the Sun's father as performers of this ceremony, while the Navajo account mentions the daughters of the Sun. See p. 11 above, and Matthews, 112.

10. Other versions make this the second naming of the elder brother. His boyhood name was "Whitehead," p. 31. Still other names are known to the Navajo. Matthews, 263-264.

11. To know by name things or animals hitherto unknown is often mentioned as a great feat. P. 24.

12. It is seldom that the Apache conception of animism is so plainly stated. Songs however abound in the designation of objects as "living."

13. When a youth went through an adolescence ceremony he did it with a definite career in mind. The normal myth of this type put the emphasis on the weapons secured and feats of warlike prowess in killing the monsters; that is, the warrior idea is uppermost. This version stresses the acquisition of horses and probably is a specialized myth for those who wish to be successful in acquiring and breeding horses.

14. The house of the Sun with the stable and corral, the furniture of the house, and many other references indicate the home of a European and such seems to be the conception.

15. The two wives of the Sun are often mentioned. The Navajo account has Esdzanadlehi go to the west where the sun visits her daily. Here and there, especially in the songs, the Moon is coupled with the Sun, and is feminine in sex. That the Moon and the Earth should both be called the "Woman who renews herself" is interesting. These conceptions are generally vague and implied rather than expressed.

16. Earth, literally "There on the earth."

17. The narrator said those mentioned at the beginning of the narrative were not real people but just like shadows. The other versions have only the one family existing at this time.

18. The reference may be to moss, especially as rain falling on it is mentioned below.

19. The narrator said it was true that horses would not pass a blanket so placed in a narrow canyon.

This order of the colors and their assignment varies from the one more generally found of black for the east and white for the south. P. 7, and Matthews, 215.

20. This announcing of names is probably to be explained as

ceremonial. Ordinarily, it is improper, probably because immodest to call one's own name.

21. The use of pollen for sacred purposes is a very important feature among the Athapascan of the Southwest. It is always preferred to the cornmeal used by the Pueblo peoples.

22. In the division of labor the women are supposed to saddle and unsaddle the horses.

23. Because he must use a white saddle, the informant explained.

24. The whinneying was heard from the top of the sky.

25. The conception of time passing while the Sun stood still is fairly difficult for a people without timepieces.

26. This method of traveling implies lightning, rainbow or a similar supernatural method, in this case said to be sunbeams.

27. The name is Naiye', "a dangerous monster," and -nezgani, "he who kills."

28. It is said above that he had no eyes in front.

29. "Mountain, its child."

30. He did not mention his fly by name.

31. Probably means he can see people who are on the opposite side of a hill.

32. These monsters are not those in the usual versions. The bringing of trophies and the narratives remind one of counting coup in the Plains. The Navajo versions also mention the bringing back of trophies.

33. One of the recognized methods of rapid locomotion.

34. The dispersion of the tribes, a common incident in origin myths.

35. The formula for the completion of a narrative.

Naiyenezgani.[36]

Long ago the Sun set and, there in the west, he became the son-in-law of Toxastinhn (Water-old-man) whose daughter he married. She, who was to become the wife of the Sun, built a house with its door facing the sunrise. She sat in the doorway facing the rising sun from which the red rays streamed toward her. These rays entered her and since her period was about to occur she became pregnant as a result.

When the child was born, its hands and feet were webbed. There was no hair on its head and it had no nose. When the boy was grown up he asked where his father lived. His mother replied that his father lived where one could not go, for the Sun was his father. The boy asked again where he lived. His mother said he lived at the sunrise, but that one could not go there. The boy then said that he would go there and set out on the journey.

He came where the cliffs come down of themselves. They moved in front of him. The lightning shot across with him. Beyond that place he came to the mountain of cactus which formed a dark barrier in front of him. There a black whirlwind twisted through for him so that he passed by. From there he went on where the mountain of mosquitoes stood like a black ridge in front of him. A female rain fell for him and the wings of the mosquitoes became damp; then he passed over. From there he went on where the mountains moved up and down toward each other. He jumped away from them and then toward them, but in no way could he get through. Black-measuring-worm, whose back is striped with lightning, bent over it with him.[37]

He walked on toward the house of the Sun. As he was going along, near sundown, a spider drew its thread across below the boy's knee and tripped him. He got up and went back, but fell again at the same place. Wondering why he had fallen, he started on again, when he saw the head of Spider-old-woman projecting from her hole so far (three inches) away. "Grandchild, where are you going?" she asked. He replied that he was going to the house of his father, the Sun. She told him to come into her house instead. He replied that the opening was too small. When assured that it was large enough, he went in. She told him one could not go to the Sun. The spider girls were lying there without skirts or shirts. They lay with the head of one toward the feet of the next. Spider-woman asked what was the piece of cloth tied to his shirt. He gave it to her and she worked with it all night; and the next morning each girl had a shirt and a skirt. She made them from the young man's piece of cloth.[38]

When the Sun rose, Spider-old-woman went out-of-doors. "It is not yet time, my grandson," she said. She held up five fingers horizontally and said it would be time when the Sun shone over them.[39] When the time came to go, they set out toward the house of the Sun. He came to the front of the house where there were twelve doors and all of them were shut. Without anyone opening a door for him, he came to Sun's wife. "What sort of a person are you?" she asked. He replied he had come to see his father. The woman warned him that no one was allowed around there. She rolled him up in a blanket,[40] which she tied with lightning, and hid him by the head of the bed.

When the sun set, he heard the noise of the Sun's arrival. The Sun came inside his house. "I do not see anyone," he said, "but from the mountain where I go down some man had gone along." "You tell me you do not have love affairs where you go around. This morning your son came here." She went to the head of the bed, undid the lightning with which he was tied up and took the boy out. The Sun saw it was his boy. There were twelve pipes in which tobacco was burned. The Sun fixed a smoke for him in one of these. It was not the Sun's proper tobacco, but a kind that killed whoever smoked it. The boy drew on the pipe just once and the tobacco was burned out. The Sun prepared another pipeful, which was gone when the boy had drawn on the pipe twice. He filled a third pipe; this time the boy drew on it three times and the tobacco was consumed. The last time the pipe was filled, the boy drew four times before the tobacco was burned out.

Toward the east, there was a blazing fire of black *yabeckon* into which the Sun threw the boy. He turned into a downy feather and landed in front of his father who expressed his surprise. There was a fire of blue *yabeckon* toward the south into which the boy was next thrown. He again turned into a feather and landed in front of his father. The fire toward the west was of yellow *yabeckon* from which the boy escaped in the same manner. Finally, the boy was thrown into a white fire of *yabeckon* which blazed up in the north. He escaped in the same manner as before. Each time when the boy was thrown in, the fire had been poked with lightning of the corresponding color.

When the boy had successfully withstood this last test, the Sun directed his wife to prepare a sweatbath. She did this by spreading four blankets of cloud: black, blue, yellow, and white. She put on the four blankets from the four sides in proper rotation. The Sun went in with all his boys. While they were in the bath, the skin between the boy's fingers and toes was pulled back and joints made in his fingers. He was also provided with hair, eyebrows, eyelashes, nose, and ears. Hair was placed on his body and nails supplied for his fingers and toes. Counting this boy, the Sun had twelve sons with whom he formed a line. He then asked his wife to find him in the line, but this she was unable to do because they all looked alike, she said.

The Sun then placed a gun and a panther-skin quiver on a shelf and asked his son to choose which he would have. After sighting the gun, he concluded he did not like it. He put the quiver over his shoulder and took out two arrows. When he tried these, he hit the target in the center. He chose the panther-skin quiver saying he liked it.[41] All the other sons of the Sun had guns. The Sun had them shoot at each other in fun. Those who had guns beat the boy who had arrows and drove him off.

On one side, horses were being made and on the other deer. The one who was in charge of making these is named Iltca'nailt'ohn.

They put, for him, a light brown mountain, inside of which, cattle, goats, sheep, pigs, horses, mules, and donkeys were living. All these are the food of white people. In this mountain also were guns, blankets, and all kinds of metals.

On the other side he put, for him, a mountain on which century plants were growing with their yellow flower stalks standing all around the edges. On this mountain, too, were sunflowers, yellow with blossoms, cactus, yucca, piñon, oaks, junipers, the fruit of all of which was perpetually ripe. All the other wild vegetable foods of the Indians grew there also. The mountain was always yellow with flowers.

The Sun asked the boy which of these two mountains he would choose. He decided to take the one which was yellow with flowers where fruit was always ripe. He did not care for the light brown mountain which stood toward the east. He announced that the yellow mountain would be his and would belong in the future to the Indians.

They then opened a door in the side of the brown mountain and drove out cattle, goats, sheep, pigs, horses, donkeys, and mules. These became the property of your white people's nation. The Sun's son asked that some horses be given him. The Sun reminded him he had asked for the other mountain, and wanted to know why he had not then asked for horses.

From the east, mirage people rounded up some horses for him. The red dust of the round-up covered the ground. "There are no horses," the Sun said. The boy asked again for horses only to be told he should have asked before when he chose between the two mountains. He asked, that notwithstanding, he be given some horses. The Sun took up a rope and led back a chestnut stallion from the east. He tied the horse which stood pawing the ground and nickering. The boy rode back on it to the place where I suppose Toxastin and his grandmother lived. He rode back in a single day and tied his horse. The horse kept nickering and pawing the earth all the time; he would not graze and the boy was not satisfied. He rode back to the house of the Sun, took off the rope; and the horse ran off toward the east kicking up his heels.

The boy told his father, the Sun, that the stallion he had given him was not satisfactory, and that he had come to ask for a different horse. His father went away and returned with two horses, a stallion and a mare. "These are what you want, I suppose," the Sun said, and gave the boy a rope, a halter, a saddle blanket, and a saddle.

The boy led the horse back to the place where Toxastin, his grandmother, and his mother lived. He led the horses back to a place called Cottonwood-branches-hang-down. To the south, blue cottonwood branches hung down; to the west, yellow cottonwood branches hung down; to the north, white cottonwood branches hung down. The place was named the center of the earth. The saddle was placed at the east; the saddle blanket at the south; the halter, at the west; and the rope, at the north.

In the dry stream bed to the east, black burdocks grew; to the south, blue burdocks grew; to the west, yellow burdocks; and to the north, white burdocks. He turned out the two horses here to the east. Each time the Sun's son came back there, he found the two horses playing. After four days, he drove the horses up the valley a little way four times. When he went the fourth day to see them he found the tracks of a colt.

That cottonwood tree stood in the center. On the east side of it a black stallion stood; on the south side, a blue stallion; on the west side, a yellow stallion; on the north side, a white stallion. Horses were walking around in the valleys to the east, south, west, and north. Thus there came to be horses here on the earth.

36. Told by the father of Frank Crockett, February, 1910. Frank's father was of the Bissaxa clan and was about sixty years old in 1910. He was still a growing youth when he left the White River country.

37. These in part are the obstacles mentioned in the Navajo account. They are overcome in a different manner. Matthews, 109-110.

38. Spider-woman is of considerable importance in the mythology of the Hopi. Voth, 2, 11. The Navajo account (Matthews, 109) omits the clothing-making episode. Spider-woman is the originator of spinning, Franciscan Fathers, 222. She is sometimes said to be the mother of the Sun and therefore Naiyenezgani's paternal grandmother.

39. An Apache method of indicating time when the Sun is near the horizon.

40. The blanket was probably a cloud. The word *caziz* ought to mean "sun-sack."

41. Had Naiyenezgani taken the gun Indians would have been armed as white men are.

The Placing of the Earth.[42]

They did not put this large one (the earth) that lies here in place before my eyes.

The wind blew from four directions. When there was no way to make the earth lie still, Gopher, who lives under the earth, put his black ropes under the earth. Here his black rope lies under it; here his blue rope; here his yellow rope; and here his white rope.

Over here (east) they made a black whirlwind stand with black metal inside of it. Here (south) a blue whirlwind and blue metal were placed; here (west) a yellow whirlwind and yellow metal; and here (north) a white whirlwind and white metal. With these standing on all sides, the earth came to its proper place and was stable.

"Now that this is as it should be, what shall we do next?" said one of them. "To what purpose have we had such a hard time making this earth lie properly which otherwise would have been unstable?" Then he began to pat it with his hand. "Let a black cloud move about sprinkling," he said.

"There will be life from this; the world will be alive from the dampness," he said. "They did well by us, what shall we do? Now thank you," they said.

The people had nothing. The one who was in charge (the Sun); that one only was walking around. "It will turn out well with him walking about," they said. They looked well at the one they meant. "That one is the Sun," they said. "We did it in the presence of that one walking about."

Then Ests'unnadli said she would do something unseemly. Thinking she would do it where the Sun first shone in the morning, she seated herself there. She was doing this only that people might live. There were no people and she thought there should be many and she did it for that reason.

She became pregnant. She and the one walking around were the only ones who understood about generation. She gave birth to a child there where she sat. She went back to the child early each morning for four mornings and on the fourth, the child walked back with her. He was entirely dressed as he walked back with her.

"It is not good that there should be only this one," she said. "It will be well for me to do an improper thing again." She sat repeatedly where the water was dripping and became pregnant again. She gave birth a second time to a child. "I will do as I did before," she said. She went to her child early each morning for four mornings. The fourth morning after he was born, the child returned with her. He was dressed in buckskin, shoes and all.

She had given birth to two children. The latter one she named Tobate'isteini and the first one Bilnajnollije.[43] They were the children of this one (the Sun).

A black water vessel by the door of the sun's house was flecked with sunshine. He caused dark lightning to dart under it from four directions. He caused it to thunder out of it in four directions. He caused it to thunder in four directions. He caused male rain to fall in four directions. He caused fruits to stand on the earth in lines pointing in four directions. "Thanks," they said, "he has treated us well."

A yellow water vessel by Ests'unnadlehi's door was flecked with light. She caused yellow lightning to pass under it from four directions. She caused it to thunder from it toward four directions. She caused female rain to fall four times in four directions. She caused fruits to stand in lines converging from four directions. "Thanks, she has treated us well," they said. "Because of her, things are well with us." "She caused the wind to agitate the grass from four directions for us," they said. "With no trouble for us it comes to its place. The earth will remain well for us," they said. "It is still the same way for us that it was long ago. We are thankful yet."

"Mother, where does our father live?" the boys asked. "Do not ask, for he lives in a dangerous place," Ests'unnadlehi replied. "Do not say he lives in a dangerous place but show us where it is, for we are going there," they replied. "If you go you must travel only by night. During the day one must sit still," she told them. She said this, for she meant for them to make the journey without being seen by the Sun.

They wondered why she told them to go only at night and resolved to travel by day. They came near where the ground was black with mosquitoes that had teeth of *becdiłxił*, and there was no way to pass through them. They caused a rain, yellow with sunshine, to fall on them and wet their wings so that they stuck to the trees. By this means, they passed beyond them. "This is why she said it is dangerous," they said to each other. They came where the earth was crossed with a stripe of cactus which had spines of *becdiłxił*. A black whirlwind with a core of *becdiłxił* passed, twisting through the cactus; the boys got by it. "This was surely the bad place of which our mother told us," they said. As they were going on toward their father's house, they came to sand which, if one stepped on it, rolled back with him. There was no way to get through it. A big black measuring worm having his back striped with a rainbow, bent himself over the sand for them and they crossed over. They were now approaching their destination when they found the house surrounded by thirty-two lakes which could not be avoided.

A turquoise bird sat in the ear of one of them and directed them on their way. The Sun's wife saw the two men pass through, avoiding the four bodies of water that surrounded the house. She concealed them under the bed which stood in the house. When the Sun returned, he saw the tracks of two men and asked where they had gone. The Sun's wife replied that they were not there. "You are always saying you have made no visits and yet your two sons come here," she said. The Sun directed that they should come to him. They sat facing him. He had tobacco hanging in sacks in four places. It was black tobacco which grew on stalks of *becdiłxił*. He had a turquoise pipe with thirty-two[44] holes for the tobacco to burn in. With this tobacco, he killed those who were not really his children. They heard him draw on the pipe once and then he tapped it on something and the ashes rolled out. "Fix me a smoke, that is why I came," one of the boys said.

They two went to the sack which was hanging on this side. It was filled with large blue tobacco which grew on stalks of *becdoł'ije*. He filled a pipe with thirty-two bowls and lighted it again. Having drawn on the pipe, he passed it to them. He heard them draw on the pipe once and then the ashes fell out.

"Prepare a smoke for me, for I came for that purpose," one of the boys said again. When the other kinds, yellow, and white had been tried from the remaining world-quarters, one of the boys produced some tobacco and a pipe made of clay with a hole through it. "This is my pipe and my tobacco," the boy announced. "Why did you not tell me before that you had tobacco?" the Sun said. He had chairs placed and took a seat between the two boys. The three looked just alike. "Come, Djingona'ai,[45] move yourself," the Sun's wife said, so that she might distinguish him from the others. "They are surely my children," the Sun declared. "What do you desire?" he asked them. The boys said they had come to hear him ask that. The Sun urged them to ask for what they wished without delay as he had many things.

Warrior Woman Tah-das-te (Dahteste)

Warrior Woman Tah-das-te (Dahteste) // The Apache is a nation of Natives who teach their boys and girls the same skills, leaving the choice of lifestyle to follow an individual decision. Girls who choose the warriors' path are not ridiculed; neither are boys who choose a gentler life – they receive equal praise if they excel in their chosen path.

The Sun had domesticated animals in four corrals on four sides of his house. He had four kinds which were bad. They were bear, coyote, panther, and wolf, of which one is afraid. He led a bear from the eastern corral, remarking that this was probably the sort they meant, that it was his pet. The boys refused it, saying they had come for his horse. In turn he led animals from corrals at the south and west which were refused each time on the advice of the monitor that sat in the ear of one of the boys. The Sun pretended he had no other horse, that he was poor. The monitor urged them to persist in their request, saying that the Sun could not refuse. He finally led to them one of the horses which was walking around unconfined. He was just skin and bones. The rope also was poor. "Did you ask for this one?" the Sun said. "That is the one," they replied. The Sun told them the horse could not travel far, but the boys said that was the animal they wanted.

He gave them the horse with the admonition that they must not let Ests'unnadlehi see it or she would send them away with it, it looked so bad. The boys assured him it would be all right. He replied that she would be surprised at least. He requested them to tell Ests'unnadlehi that he, the Sun, always told the truth. He charged the two boys that they should not lie to each other. "This is a good day for you both," he told them. "Thank you, Ests'unnadlehi, my mother, thanks." "Thank you, Djingona'ai, my father. It is true that it is fortunate for us. It was for that reason you raised us," they said.[46]

42. Told in 1910 by a very dignified man, C. G. 2, of about sixty years. He is a leader of the Naiyenezgani songs used for adolescent girls.

43. The lightning strikes with him, evidently a poetic name.

44. It was explained that four was the real number, thirty-two being presumably a ceremonial or poetic exaggeration.

45. "Goes by day," the Sun.

46. This fragment of the culture-hero story having been told, the narrator refused to proceed, perhaps because he knew it had already been several times recorded.

The Adolescence Ceremony.[47]

The Sun was the one who arranged the ceremony for unclean women. She (Ests'unnadlehi) sat thus on her knees and the red light from the sun shone into her. She was living alone.

The Apache sunrise ceremony came about from the myth of the White Painted Woman, which is passed on from generation to generation in Apache storytelling. Called the "Na'ii'ees", the Apache Sunrise Ceremony is a four-day communal celebration that marks the first moon cycle of an Apache woman. It consists of numerous sacred rituals, dances, songs, and enactments during which the girl becomes a living representation of White Painted Woman, the first woman in the world and the mother of the Apache people (Yupanqui 1999).

The purposes of the Sunrise ceremony are numerous. First, a young woman undergoing the ceremony achieves a deep connection to her spiritual heritage. She identifies with White Painted Woman and the symbol of divine womanhood that she represents. Second, it marks the transition from childhood to adulthood, allowing the young woman to celebrate her new status in a communal setting. Third, it helps her embrace her role as an Apache woman, encouraging her to be hard working, selfless, and composed. According to Tika Yupanqui, the young woman's "temperament during the ceremony is believed to be the primary indicator of her temperament throughout her future life". Finally, the Sunrise ceremony helps unify the community by bring friends and families together (Yupanqui 1999). The hosting of a Sunrise ceremony can sometimes require up to six months of preparation. The young woman undergoing the ceremonial ordeal must be trained, her buckskin dress must be sewed, a medicine man must be chosen, food must be prepared, and a hundred other large and small tasks must be completed simply for the Sunrise ceremony to begin (Yupanqui 1999).

When she becomes a woman they straighten her. The people stand in a line and sing while the drum is beaten. They dance four nights. They paint her with white clay that she may live a long time, and that her hair may get white on one side of her head. They put up a cane with a curved top for her around which she is to run. At one side a basket stands in which there is tobacco and on the other side a basket containing corn.

When she has run around the cane in its first position, it is put up again farther away, where she runs around it again and returns to the line of singers. Again, the cane and basket of corn are moved out and the girl runs around them. When she returns to the singers she dances, having a downy feather tied at the crown of her head. The cane is put up again and the basket of corn moved once more. The girl runs around them returning to the singers. This cane is said to be the sun's cane and the chief's cane.

The corn is poured from the basket over the crown of the girl's head. The people all try to get a handful of the corn. After that, she throws the blankets in every direction and the people pick them up, saying, "May her blankets be many." They plant the corn and all say they raise large crops in consequence.

They prepare Gans and dance four nights. They do not allow anyone to sleep during the dancing.

The girl, Ests'unnadlehi, has a skirt and a shirt of dressed skin. The shirt is spoken of as fringed shirt and the skirt, a fringed skirt.

When the Gans dance, the girl dances behind them. She does not sleep during the four nights.

On the morning after the fourth night all the people gather around to insure good luck in the future. The sun's songs, the chief's songs, are sung and with them they dance. After the four nights they paint the girl white with gypsum mixed with water which is in a shallow basket. The girl stands here and a woman whose husband is rich in horses and other property stirs the gypsum and water with a hairbrush. She applies this white mixture to the girl's head, and brushes her downward until she is whitened all over. The girl then sprinkles the men, women, and children who stand around in a large circle. This is done that they may be fortunate in the future. If some of the white mixture falls on the hair, that person will have gray hair at that spot.

47. Told by Frank Crockett's father in part, and extended by Frank who was interpreting.

The Migration of the Gans.[48]

They say they moved about from place to place under the cliffs. "We will move to a place where we will not die," they said. They went to a place halfway between the earth and sky, and lighted on a mirage. They were dying there too. They came back to this world. Wind and rain ceased.

Mocking bird said he wanted to be chief. Gopher said he wanted to be chief. When someone remarked that the chief's eyes were small, Gopher was angry and went under the ground, taking with him the wind and rain.

Humming bird started over the earth, hunting in vain for the wind and rain. He came where Gopher had gone underground and went in there and came where the Gans were living. They had much corn and ripe crops. It rained there all the time. Humming bird came back and reported that he had been where there were many ripe crops and where rain fell all the time. He also said those who live there do not die. The Gans started to move down there and on their way came to a place called "Two-mountains-go-around-each-other-in-opposite-directions." Rocks, white and all colors, lie there, one above the other. The Indians went there and came where the Gans were living.

A small mountain stood at the east and on it Black Gan stood every dawn and talked as a chief. When he had spoken as chief four mornings, they asked why Black Gan was talking that way. All the Gans came together and he talked to them. "May one of your children remain here?" he asked. All the Gans said, "No. Our children are all going with us." Then Black Gan decided that one of his should stay. He left the youngest little girl, putting a turquoise water jar by her pillow. He covered this with earth. They started away where people do not die. His little girl returned to the place where her water jar had been put. While she was gone for it the others moved away and left her.

Some Indians found the baby, who was running about crying, and took her to raise. When she was grown, she married, and gave birth to a boy. Then Black Gan had a son-in-law and many people came to see him because he was Black Gan's son-in-law. They crowded into the house and kept saying, "Move over a little, Donaildihi." He, Eats-a-long-time-without-being-satisfied, moved over; and they kept coming in until the house was stretched over to one side.

Black Gan's son-in-law lay down with one leg over the other, and called for the baby. When its grandmother brought it, he tossed it up and down on his chest and sang to it. When he was done playing with it, he called to them to take it again.

After a time another boy was born. When they were both grown they were hunting birds and came where the Gans were living. When they returned, food was offered them in vain. They had eaten where the Gans lived while away, and would not eat on their return.

A man fell sick. His eyes and mouth were crooked, as were also his arms and legs. The people were asking what they should do about it. The man told the mother of the boys to prepare a deerskin which had no holes in it with a piece of turquoise fastened at the forehead. To the turquoise he asked that downy feathers be tied. She directed that *bacinϵ* with downy feathers be tied between the eyes. In addition *tsϵltcϵϵ* and *yoɫgai* each with downy feathers were to be tied to the skin. She asked that the skin prepared thus be placed on the top of the feet of the children (Gan's grandchildren).

When they put it on the foot of one of these boys, he kicked it to the other boy, who kicked it back. When this had been done four times one of them directed that wood be brought in, and they consented to give a dance for the sick man. They directed that all the people should come together and that the sick man should be brought to the dancing place. Preparations were also made there for the fire. "All of you come here where we are going to sing," they announced.

When they had come together they began to sing, the two grandsons of Black Gan acting as leaders. When they started to dance one of them stood up and made a speech. He told them they must not go away during the dance or something bad would happen to them.

When they had sung four songs, the sound of a bull roarer was heard underground to the east, south, west, and north. The Gans ran there and formed in line around him (the sick man). The Gans came to the dance ground, and Black Gan shook himself by the side of the sick man. He took the sick man up and threw him over there. Then Brown Gan shook his body by the sick man and swayed from side to side. Then the Gan who has one side of his face covered, shook himself by the sick man and threw him over there. Next Red Gan swayed himself and took up the sick man and threw him over there.

The Black Gan then went to the sick man and made his eyes good again. Brown Gan went to him and fixed his arms. The Gan whose face is half covered fixed his back. On this side (north) Red Gan restored his legs. The man was well again, and danced among the others. They danced four nights and the morning after, the Gans and men stood with their little fingers interlocked; first a man and then a Gan; a man and then a Gan; a man and then a Gan. Thus they formed a circle, standing in a line alternating, with their little fingers interlocked. They danced until it grew light and then the dance began to move away toward the sunrise. Old men and old women were lying down nearby. The dancing people kept moving away toward the east. The old women and old men ran after them. They were dancing on the ground and then began to move up higher and higher in the air. The Indians ran after them but the Indians who were dancing went up with the dance. They could hear the sound of the dancing up there and the songs. They moved away to the Sun. He sent them where they do not die. They are still living there, I suppose. They are the people who do not die.

48. Told by the father of Frank Crockett, February, 1910.

Releasing the Deer.[49]

Ganisk'ide[50] was the only one who owned deer. He was the only one who brought them home and who ate their flesh. He gave none of the meat to the people who lived near him.

Apache Scout

Ravens, who were then people, proposed that they make a puppy and desert it. They did this; they moved away and left a puppy lying there. When the children of Ganisk'ide went where the people had moved away, they found the puppy. They took it up and carried it home.

Ganisk'ide told the children to throw the puppy away, but when they objected, he told them to try the dog's eyes by holding fire in front of them. When they brought the fire near the dog's eyes it cried, "gai gai gai." "It is a real dog," Ganisk'ide said. "You may take him behind the stone door where the deer are enclosed and let him eat the entrails."

When the children had taken the dog behind this door he became a man again. He moved the stone to one side and the deer that were inside ran out. Ganisk'ide called to his wife from the doorway to touch the nostrils of the deer with her odorous secretions. She touched each of the deer on the nose as they ran by her and they received the sense of smell.

They ran away from her.

"You said it was a dog," he said to his children with whom he was angry, "but he turned them out for us." The deer scattered all over the earth.

49. Told by the father of Frank Crockett.

This is a very widely distributed tale. The owner of the animals is usually Raven or Crow. See this series, vol. 8, 212-4; Russell, 259; Wissler and Duvall, 50-53; Kroeber, 65; this series, vol. 10, 250-251.

50. Ganisk'ide is a deity known to the Navajo, Matthews, 37, 244.

Deer Woman.[51]

After he married, they went on a hunting trip. When they had established camp where they were to get the deer meat, the man went out to hunt, but the woman stayed at the camp. As the husband left, he said, if anyone came from the north, that would be himself, but if someone came from the east it would be someone else.

Then Ganłjine came there carrying a deer mask in his hand which he put on the brush of which the camp was made, and sat down by the fire. The deer mask was eating as if it were alive and it made a noise like a deer. Ganłjine told the woman to put on the thing which was lying there. She replied that a deer mask was something to be afraid of. "Put it on and let me look at it," he insisted. "Will it be all right?" she asked him. He told her to put it on anyway, and stand at one side so he could look at it. She put it on and stood at the place designated in the posture of a deer.

He threw a turquoise ring on her, and she became like a deer as far as her neck. Then he threw a ring of *bacinɛ* on her and an additional portion of her body changed to a deer. Next he threw a ring of *tcɛltcɛɛ*, and last, one of *yołgai*. She was then completely like a deer and walked away, wiggling her tail.

Toward the east there are mountains called Iłijgo. There are four mountains standing in a line, one back of the other. She who used to be a woman and Ganłjine went there together. They were mating as they went along, as could be told from the tracks. Deer tracks were in one place and nearby, other deer tracks, but on one side a man's tracks. They went toward the east.

Deer Woman is a shape-shifting woman in Native American mythology. She allegedly appears at various times as an old woman, or a young beautiful maiden,

When the husband came back he saw by the tracks that a man had visited the camp and had gone away with his wife. He went back to the settlement and told them that the woman with whom he had gone to hunt had gone off, leaving human tracks on one side and on the other side like a deer.

The people went in a company to the place where the man had camped and commenced following the tracks that were human on one side and deer-like on the other. While being trailed they ran from those who were following them, who ran after them, chasing them around until the one who had been a woman was worn out. They overtook her and threw on her a ring of turquoise, followed by one of *bacinε* and then one of *tcεɬcεε*, and finally one of *yoɬgai*. As these rings fell on her she became progressively human in shape. When she had become a human being again, they took her back to the settlement. When it was time for deer to run again, she became a deer once more, and then became a person again.

When thunder was heard, they made a camp and went to hunt little fawns which they were bringing into the camp. This woman who had turned into a deer had little fawns which she had borne for a deer. She went around among the houses where the fawns were being brought in and found her own lying there dead. An Indian had killed them both and had brought them in. When she learned a man had brought in pretty fawns, with yellow around their eyes, she ran there and commenced to cry.

She spoke, saying that the deer they should see along the trail where she went with her children would be herself and that they should pray to her.

51. Told by Frank Crockett's father following the preceding story so closely as to make its separation a matter of doubt. A fuller version was obtained from San Carlos.

The Gambler who secured the Water-Ceremony.[52]

A boy started playing *najonc* and lost his arrows, his moccasins, his breechcloth, his shirt, his headband, his hair, his eyebrows, and his eyelashes. When he returned home so divested, his mother told him to go away somewhere that she might not see him again.

He started away, utterly naked as he was, and traveled until he came to the edge of the ocean. He jumped into the water but was thrown back.[53] He did this three times with the same result and then jumped in under the water. When he looked back through the water it was white. He began to eat all kinds of "worms" as he went along. He ate, also, some of the green growth floating on the water. They came with him to the house made of water. The fly that sat inside his ear gave him information and advice. All the water people and the fog people went with him; Water-old-man was among them and Water-youth with a downy feather on the crown of his head. He was sent down that way with a message.[54] They sent him where the black blanket of water is spread down.

"Over there he is running along," someone said. "Now to you they are starting, Water-youths, to you they are starting. Yonder we are coming, Water-youths are coming," he said. "They are coming right up the stream.

"Fog-youths are coming, right in front of the fog they are coming.

"Where the water stands straight up, next to him, the water people are coming to us. With water-downy-feathers as their feathers they are coming to us; holding the lightning in their hands they are coming to us.

"Where the fog stands straight up, standing next to me, they come to us," he said. "Fog-youths come to us," he said. "At the end of the water, they come to us. Having downy feathers of fog they come to us; holding the lightning in their hands they come to us."[55]

The one who became water came by the house made of fog and water. "Where is the place called 'House-of-water'?" he asked. "This place is called 'House-of-water'" the water people replied. His monitor, fly, told him they were not telling him the truth. He came to the house made of water. "Where is the place called 'House-of-water'?" he asked. It was Water Chief to whom he came. "It is called 'Water-house' right here," he replied. His fly told him that was correct; that 'Water-house' was there.

Two vessels filled with water which was boiling, were by the fire. "Drink all there is in one of the vessels," he was told by Water Chief. He drank the contents of one vessel and then vomited. He was saying, "wa, wa," as he vomited. He threw up all of the underwater "worms."

They bathed him with the contents of the other vessel. They commenced to dance and danced for twelve nights without sleeping. When they had danced twelve nights without his falling asleep they told him he might go home.

Then Naiyenezgani danced there among them. His hat was white on top. He held his hand outspread over him as he stood by him. Water-old-man, too, danced among them. Water-house was on this side.

"Water-youths all came here where they were dancing. With their downy feathers of water they came there. They came to the dance ground holding lightning in their hands.

"From 'House-made-of-fog,' Fog-girls came where they danced

having their downy feathers of fog. They held lightning in their hands.

"Water-youths were behind them, pretty, they were behind them; having their downy feathers of water, they were behind them. Holding lightning in their hands, they were all behind them.

"The Fog-girls came from the house made of fog. Having downy feathers of fog, they danced with fog. All holding lightning in their hands, the dance being made of fog they started to dance with him.

"They danced with the boy who became water."

Naiyenezgani danced among them. When they were looking somewhere else Naiyenezgani became a baby again, and was tied in a basket cradle. The attention of the people was attracted elsewhere and when they saw Naiyenezgani again he was standing among the Water-maidens to whom he did various things.

Tobatc'istcini, too, was tied as a baby, then the two men did various things to them. The twelve nights had passed without anyone sleeping. He stood between the Water-maidens. The men from a distance made a circle and danced. The Water-people danced with him. The Fog-people danced with him.

Tonto Apache Woman, taken at the San Carlos Indian Reservation. She is not identified

55

The Sun was present there. From so great a height[56] he looked down on them. They danced in his presence. They danced, too, in the presence of the Moon. When twelve nights had passed and it was the twelfth morning he went to sleep. Far off, a Water-maiden stood. He, who became water, stood here and there stood a Fog-maiden. When twelve nights had passed he fell asleep. He loved this one. They shouted to him saying, "You are falling asleep." The one standing behind him stepped by his foot and he fell against him.

Bił'olisn was there where they were dancing. "He took her away, where the land is beautiful with corn. "Fog-maiden; where the land is beautiful with pumpkins. "Bił'olisn; where the land is beautiful with large corn, they two went. "Fog-maiden; where the land is beautiful with large pumpkins, they two went. "Bił'olisn; where the land is beautiful with large corn, they two sat down. "Fog-maiden; where the land is beautiful with large pumpkins, they two sat down. "Bił'olisn; where the land is beautiful with large corn, they two lay down. "Fog-maiden; where the land is beautiful with pumpkins, they two lay down.

"At the east where the black water lies, stands the large corn, with staying roots, its large stalk, its red silk, its long leaves, its tassel dark and spreading, on which there is dew.

"At the sunset, where the yellow water lies, stands the large pumpkin with its tendrils, its long stem, its wide leaves, its yellow top on which there is pollen."[57]

This all happened where the man turned to water. He came back here where people were living. His mother had her hair cut off and was weeping for him. He came back at the end of a year. His younger brother was walking outdoors and saw him. When he saw him coming back he said, "Mother, over there my brother is returning." "Evil one,[58] why do you say that?" she replied. "I am telling the truth, my brother is coming. Come here and look," the boy said. She came out and found it was true. She called him her son, and told him she had been having a hard time and had cried on his account.

He went and hunted deer in company with his brother. He asked his brother to hunt in a certain direction and circle around to him again. There were thunder showers. The young man was sitting by himself. In one direction it was raining, it was black with the falling rain.

"I wish I might drink water again on top where black rain stands up. I wish I might drink water again on top where the water stands up." His brother returned and surprised him while he was still singing.

They went back again to the house and the boy told them that his brother had been singing. He was told there were no songs and that he was not speaking the truth. He reaffirmed his statement. He asked that a sweathouse be built. When it was ready the boys went in and were singing inside. The young man who had been turned into water started to sing the water songs. Inside he wove lightning together again. There had been no water songs and now they existed. Thus, there came to be medicinemen for water.

52. Told by Frank Crockett's father who practised the ceremony. It is for the recovery of those who have been made ill by the floods due to thunderstorms.

53. A gambler made desperate by his losses is the hero of a Navajo (Matthews, 160) and a Jicarilla story (This series, vol. 8, 214).

54. A messenger wears a downy feather tied at the crown of his head and is protected by it on his journey. It serves as a safe conduct.

55. These four paragraphs appear to contain the words of songs.

56. As high as a man's head.

57. Clearly a song.

58. Because one supposedly dead was being mentioned to a near relative.

The Man who visited the Sky with the Eagles.[59]

Long ago, there was a man who had a wife and two children, both boys. He went with Coyote on a hunting trip and camped near where they expected to secure game. He went out to hunt in the morning; and Coyote also went by himself and, as he was walking along, he came where there was an eagle's nest on a point of rock jutting out in the middle of a high cliff. There were young eagles in the nest.

Coyote returned to the camp and reported to the hunter that he had seen young eagles in a nest. Saying he wished some good feathers for feathering arrows, he asked the other man to lower him from the top of the cliff to the nest. When they had come to the place, Coyote asked the other man to allow himself to be lowered and to throw the feathers down for him. Coyote lowered him, asking if he had come to the young eagles. The reply was, "Not yet." A little later, the same question was repeated and the answer this time was, "Yes." Coyote then let the rope fall on the man saying, "Cousin, she who was your wife will be mine."

The man then sat with the young eagles. He asked what sort of weather prevailed when their father returned. They replied that a "male" rain fell.[60] Soon a "male" rain fell and the father of the young eagles flew back in the rain. When he came where the man was sitting with the young eagles, he asked who was there. The man replied that Coyote had lowered him and that he was hovering his children for him. The male bird told him he might remain there and flew off.

The man then asked the young birds in what sort of weather their mother came back. They said she returned when a "female" rain was falling. Soon a "female" rain fell and the eagle's wife returned. She asked the man who he was; he told her that Coyote had lowered him down there and that he was staying with her children. Now she told him he might remain there and departed.

The male bird came back accompanied by a "male" rain. He brought with him a water vessel made of turquoise and bade the man drink. He drank and the water was not exhausted although the vessel of turquoise was very small.[61]

Accompanied by a "female" rain the female bird returned and perched nearby. She put down a horn vessel of boiled corn and invited the man to eat it. It was a small vessel, but it was not empty when he had finished his meal.

She flew away again and after four days the eagle people all assembled. They gave him an eagle shirt and instructed him to do as they did. He put on the shirt and flew a little way with it. He put on one shirt after another and flew farther and farther each time, four times. He was a man but he became an eagle.

"Where am I going?" he asked. "Where the black mirage is located at the center of the sky, I go up. In the shadow of his dark wings, I come. "Where the blue mirage is located at the center of the sky, I go up. In the shadow of his blue wings, I come. "Where the yellow mirage is located at the center of the sky, I go up. In the shadow of the yellow wings, I come. "Where the white mirage is located at the center of the sky, I go up. In the shadow of the white wings, I come," he sang. "Between the two who sit on the white sky, I go up. Where the white weeds tower up, white on the sky at its center, I go up," he sang. "Where the dark houses of the eagles project, I come," he sang. "Where the blue houses of eagles project, I go up. "Where the red houses of the eagles project, I go up. "Where the white houses of the eagles project, I go up," he sang.

He lay down where there were no habitations. They asked him in vain to come inside the building, for soon the person with a skull that kills would come.

Saying he would remain there, he refused, and lay down. In the night, he heard the one with a skull that kills coming. He took up a stone and hit him with it as he walked by and killed him. He also killed the bees that had caused the eagles to die out by stinging them. He took the bees from their nests and killed them all. He killed, too, the wasps that lived in rocks, and all the yellow jackets. The tumble weeds, also, were killing the eagles by rolling on them. He beat these weeds with a stick and destroyed them.

Woman with Eagle and Wolf

He inquired of an old eagle woman where others were living. She told him of wood-rats which have many houses and bring back much material when they go abroad. He went where cactus was standing and when night came, lay down to sleep. He heard the sound of people shouting toward the east. They were saying, "Down here." They were chasing an insect called *agetdlic*. He killed it.

The stars were people and were coming to get arrows. Those who were running after *agetdlic* jumped over his body one by one as they reached it. The last one who was running succeeded in jumping over the body but fell back on it.

They removed the skin, cut up meat, tied it up, and put it on the man's back for him to carry. They warned him against looking back. He started away with it and carried it until he came to the top of a hill. Wondering why he had been told not to look back, he did so and fell over backward. He went to the camp of the eagles and told them his load was on the hill. They went to get the load and brought it to the camp. There was a big pile of the meat which they brought back. "This was what he meant," they said. It was sunset by the time they brought the meat back.

"The man is a good helper," they said. "He has killed for us all those who used to kill us." The man then said he was going home, and the eagle people told him he might do so. They told him, though, that if he was afraid four times to fly down, that he could not go down. He was afraid the fourth time and came back saying that he would start home again on the fourth day.

They went with him to the place where the trail came up. He was afraid three times, but when it was to be the fourth time he flew down.

"Where the white mirage is located in the center of the sky he rested; where the yellow house stands, resting in its shadow he sat down.

"The blue house, standing at the center of the sky; resting in the shade he sat down again.

"The black house, standing at the center of the sky; resting in its shade he sat down again."

From there he flew down and lit on the earth. He alighted on a tree near which sat the Coyote who had lowered him. He was saying he would shoot the eagle there and get feathers to fix his arrow's. When Coyote tried to steal up close under him the eagle flew away to his house and became a man again. Those, who used to be his children had been renamed, "They grew up by eating the neck." Coyote had punched their eyes out. "He did it with an awl," they told their father.

When he came back from hunting, his two children had been all right. He heard him bring his load as he came back. He was saying, "Raised-with-neck-meat, come and meet me." "Do not go there," he told his sons. Coyote kept shouting as he came. He brought the load there and threw it down. He called out. "Good, Cousin. You have come back? I took good care of your children."

The man who had been with the eagles then told his wife to put four stones on the fire. She put them on the fire to heat. She put one here and one here. "Put two of the stones in your mouth and put your feet on these two," he told Coyote. Coyote did as he was told to, but ran only a little way before his tail fell out. His wife had an ill odor from being with Coyote. He beat among Coyote's children with a stick.

He did not like living on the earth. He placed eagle plumes in a row which multiplied fourfold. With the aid of these the man became an eagle. The people living here came to have medicinemen with power from eagles. He was a man but became an eagle and is now in the sky above.

59. Told by the father of Frank Crockett in February, 1910. For the distribution of this story see p. 67 above. It was said to be the myth of a ceremony used to cure one who gets ill from eagle feathers when he uses them to put on his arrows.

60. This method of knowing when the parents are to return is found in another myth, p. 17 above.

61. A similar supplying of his wants is in the Navajo account, Matthews, 199.

He who became a Snake.[62]

A man (Naiyenezgani) was living alone. He brought wood there and built a fire. He danced on rawhide against white men and then went to war. He came where the white people were and killed a white woman. He raised up her skirt with a stick and Gila monster was there. "Let that be your name," he said and Gila Monster was called łenellai. The two of them started back and came to a mountain called Bitcilł'ehe. From there they went back and came to a place called Tsitena'a. A porcupine was there and one of the men said, "My cousin, a porcupine lies here." They killed it and buried it in the ashes of the fire. At midnight he uncovered it, but Naiyenezgani did not eat of it, only his partner. "My cousin, it tastes like red peppers, taste it," he said. They lay down again and went to sleep. The next morning there were traces where the one who had eaten had crawled into the water as a snake. Naiyenezgani went back from there and in the yellow light of evening came back to Tatakawa,[63] saying, "Since early this morning I came from Tsitena'a." When all the people had come together they asked, "What place is called that?" "Big-hawk-old-man says he has been all over earth and seen everything.[64] Send for him," they said. When he was summoned, he came walking with his cane and sat down. "You are accustomed to say you have seen every place on earth. A man says he has come from Tsitena'a since early this morning," they told him. "Well, it is not near. I flew from there in ten days and when I came here the yellow light of sunset was over the earth."

Naiyenezgani then said, "He stayed with me last night and he ate something. It seems he turned into a snake and crawled in the river."

All the Eagle people, Black Whirlwind, the Sun, the Moon, and the Gan people all started toward Tsitena'a. When they came there, in the presence of the Sun and Moon, Black Gan rolled a turquoise hoop into the water. The water of the river rose up so much. Then Ganłbaiye rolled a hoop of *bacinε* into the water. Next Gan with his face half covered rolled a hoop of *tsɛłtcɛɛ* in the water and the river was lifted up so much (about a yard). Finally, Ganłtci' rolled a hoop of *yołgai* and the water was high enough above the river bed that a man could walk under it.[65]

They all entered the bed of the river and followed the man who had turned into a snake. They finally overtook him. There was a snake on the other side which they concluded was the one who had been a man. A turquoise hoop was rolled toward him and it jumped over his neck. From the neck up he took on the appearance of a man. A hoop of *bacinε* was next rolled and it fell to the waist. Next a loop of *tcɛłtcɛɛ* was rolled which jumped on the man and fell to the hips, above which he took the form of a man. Finally a hoop of *yołgai* was rolled, and his entire body became human. Then they took him by the hand and led him back. They danced for him twelve nights and he was restored as a man. During the twelve nights, no one was allowed to sleep, but someone did fall asleep. The one who had turned into a snake began to sing, "I am going up. I am going up where the sky comes together," he said as he sang. He was no longer seen where he had been standing. The man had a sister who began to sing. "Truly, I am going where it is called, mesquites-come-together." She was no longer where she had been standing.

She is the one who crawls around here in the summertime. The female lives below; the male lives above.[66]

It was here the Indians secured the supernatural power. Naiyenezgani alone had the *najonc* poles. He alone played with them. There were two of the poles.

My yucca fruits lie this way.

62. Told by the father of Frank Crockett in February, 1910. This is the myth upon which the ceremony for curing one bitten by a snake rests. For the San Carlos version see p. 64 above.

63. A valley on Cedar Creek in the White Mountain country.

64. This knowledge of geography by a bird-old-man is found in a San Carlos story, p. 21.

65. The deities and materials have definite associations with the world-quarters. There are certain variations in this association.

66. This refers to rattlesnakes under the mesquite bushes where they are said to be frequently encountered. The male above is probably the lightning which from this narrative appears connected with the porcupine.

The Hunter who secured the Bear Ceremony.[67]

A man was out hunting when there was snow on the ground. As he walked along a hillside he slipped and fell off. Below was a bear's den and he fell right into it. When the female bear discovered him she jumped around and said, "Wau, wau, wau, wau." "Please do not act like that, grandmother," he said. "It seems I fell in here." He remained there four days without anything to eat. "Are you not hungry?" the bear asked. "I am hungry," he replied, "but what is there I can eat?" She shook herself and cactus fruit rained down from her. After a second period of fasting, the same question was asked and the same reply given. When the bear shook herself, juniper berries fell. The third time it was white oak acorns, and the fourth time, manzanita berries.

After that she said there were two persons living across the valley and that they would go there to visit. She also said the visit would be dangerous, for she had in mind bears and a bear's camp. The bear told the man to remain between her hind legs during the period of danger.

When they entered the bear's house and the hosts became aware of the man's presence, they became aroused and growled, "Wau, wau, wau." The man remained between the hind legs of his companion who reached around with her front legs and defended him. "He has been with me a long time and he is our friend," she said to the others.

Next they all went to a camp where there were three bears and there again the same things happened and the same expressions were used. From there they went with him to a camp where there were four bears. He was protected at that camp as on the former occasions and was introduced as a friend.

Accompanied by the bears, he went back to the camp at which he had first arrived. He had been gone a year. He came back to his own people. From this man there came to be bear songs and medicinemen with bear power.

67. Told by the father of Frank Crockett in February, 1910.

The Cannibal Owl.[68]

Owl was a person. He lived by eating people, carrying off the small children in a large burden basket. He had a wife to whom he brought them, saying to her, "Boil them." When they were cooked he ate them.

There were some people who were living in a large house made of white cactus. Owl poked a pole in after them. The people inside held on to the pole. Owl pulled on it and the people held to it. They let go suddenly and Owl fell over backwards. He took two children on his back and carried them away toward the camp. He put the basket down with the children in it and went some distance away to urinate. While he was gone, the children put a large stone in the basket and defiled it. Owl started away again with his load, but when he passed under the limb of a tree the children caught hold of it. They turned into downy feathers and were blown away by the wind. "Boys, downy feathers are being blown about over there," he said. They had been persons, but now they were downy feathers. Owl brought his load to the house for his wife. She took a knife and tried to cut across the stone with it. "It is a stone," she said. He took it to his son-in-law. "It is a stone with manure on it," he said. "That is its gall," he replied. Owl went back to his wife. (The story was interrupted at this point.)

68. Told by the father of Frank Crockett, February, 1910.

The Doings of Coyote.[69]

Long ago, Coyote was told that the people were dying. He tied together a hairbrush, a wooden skin-dresser, and a stone pestle, and threw them in the water. "If these float let them come back to life," he said. They sank and, therefore, the dead did not come back.[70]

Snow fell. It rained down in the form of flour. This same Coyote said, "I chewed ice," and it became ice.

Also the horns of deer were tallow. Coyote again said, "I chew bones."

Coyote became ill. He had a handsome daughter. When he became ill, he told his wife to throw him away. He said their daughter was to be given to a man with a panther-skin quiver on his back who would come to play *najonc*. This man, he said, would also have a prairie-dog in his hand.

When Coyote was dead his wife gave the daughter to the man described by Coyote and he married her. It was Coyote himself, who married his own daughter. He had her hunt his lice. On the back of his head was a large wart. He told her that the lice always stay on this side, indicating a portion of his head remote from the wart. While she was looking for his lice, her husband fell asleep. Wondering why he always spoke as he did, she looked on the back of his head. There was a wart there. She slipped his head off her lap while he was asleep and going to her mother told her that the man was her father; that he had a wart on the back of his head. She picked up a large stone and was about to strike him on the crown of his head when he saw her shadow. He jumped, ran out, and trotted off toward the east. Whenever he came where there were camps people reviled him as the man who had his own daughter for his wife. They heard him saying "ci, ci, ci." They referred to him as the scabby one and hit him. He cried "wai" and turned from human form into a coyote.

Coyote was driving some mules. He smothered five of the mules. He wondered what smothered them. "Hurry," he said, "skin their throats. This place will be called Coyote Springs," he said.

When coyotes were people they all drank whiskey and ran about everywhere shouting. When they became coyotes, they barked.

69. Told by the father of Frank Crockett.

70. This incident is generally known over western North America. Professor Boas has discussed its distribution.

Bibliography.

Franciscan Fathers, The. An Ethnologic Dictionary of the Navaho Language. St. Michaels, Arizona, 1910. Goddard, Pliny Earle, (a) Jicarilla Apache Texts (Anthropological Papers, American Museum of Natural History, vol. VIII. New York, 1911.)   (b) The Beaver Indians (Anthropological Papers, American Museum of Natural History, vol. X, part IV. New York, 1916.) Kroeber, A. L. Gros Ventre Myths and Tales (Anthropological Papers, American Museum of Natural History, vol. I, part III. New York, 1907.) Matthews, Washington. Navaho Legends (Memoirs, American Folk-Lore Society, vol. V. New York, 1897.) Russell, Frank. Myths of the Jicarilla Apache (Journal of American Folk-Lore, vol. XI, 1898.) Voth, H. R. The Traditions of the Hopi (Publication 96, Anthropological Series, Field Columbian Museum, vol. VIII. Chicago, 1905.) Wissler, Clark, and Duvall, D. C. Blackfoot Mythology (Anthropological Papers, American Museum of Natural History, vol. II, part I. New York, 1908.) **TRANSCRIBER'S NOTES**

www.ingramcontent.com/pod-product-compliance
Lightning Source LLC
Chambersburg PA
CBHW081854280526
45789CB00007B/2689